side street poems

elliot m rubin

Paperback ISBN 978-1-962374-23-1
EBook   ISBN 978-1-962374-24-8

Library of Congress Control Number 2024911823

Published by Prolific Pulse Press LLC
Raleigh, North Caroline USA

Publication Date: June 2024

Dedication

To my grandchildren
Shane, Isabelle, Jonathan, Carter,
Alexandra, Melanie, Mollie, and Madison

In memory of my father
Herman S. Rubin
who wrote poetry and prayers all his life

Preface

I believe poetry is to be read and understood by all, and it needs to be written, for the most part, in plain language for everyone's enjoyment.

Too often, poets write in-depth, penetrating poems where you need to be well-read and/or versed in literary minutia to appreciate the poetry; not this book or any of my writings. I try to write so everyone can enjoy a few moments of intellectual satisfaction without consulting a dictionary or encyclopedia all the time.

Table of Contents

September 11 memorial

how many times must we read names
how many tears must we shed
how many children lost a parent
how many years must we remember
how many days is forever

fate

years ago,
i played piano
for the angel of death
as he waited in the rear
of the inner-city
public school auditorium
before selections began

shrouded in darkness
life ends suddenly
you never know
when the hand of finality
touches a shoulder

family and friends
grieve
death has no sensibility
it collects its quota
regardless
i remember
those innocents

their future
before them
as darkness
strolls the aisles

first love

more than a reunion dance
fifty years had passed
since they last held each other
her hand gently placed
near his neck
his on her waist to pull close
old bodies touching
s l o w l y   they dancedtogether
memories of seventeen-year-olds
flash to the present

spouses forgotten
teenage love *simmers* once more
and with maturity
the burners are turned down
they enjoy the moment for what it is
a return to what once was
yet will never flame again

mattress store poems

1 - hollywood

a grey-haired woman entered my mattress store
she wants to buy a firm one for herself
it's been years since my husband bothered
then she smiles at me
                and tilts her head

i don't know american sign language
but she sent a message loud and clear–
in her senior years, thin, energetic, braless
a petite chest poked out from a sheer blouse

since i am almost eighty and married
i thought, what would bogart do
there was no piano player in the room
or a smoke-filled cabaret with people near me

i look for an airplane for her to leave on
or gendarmes with guns to check a passport–
it came down to me and her alone in a store
and *these are what dreams are made of* *

*Sam Spade from The Maltese Falcon™ motion
picture 1941 by Warner Brothers™ studios.

2 - claire

i didn't think you'd return
when you offered your body
rejected by a husband
elderly and neutered

your smile behind a mask
betrayed by your bright eyes
a soothing vocal tone with
a lithe figure, energetic yet stalled

desire floats with your words
i sense your body shake
it waits to be let loose
now shackled, strained, unyielding
to throbbing urges

your pot simmers
waits to be stirred
liquids to be tasted
a meal to be devoured
enjoyed by both

i didn't think you'd return

3 - almost

she wants more
her husband offers her less
unsaid messages
transmitted through thoughtful
actions
imply desire

i didn't ask why
i knew what she did imply
i was willing

yet

her blouse now buttoned
she left
            without comment

4 - conjugal

do me, i asked you to do me she said
    but I'm married
i want you, don't you see
    really, are you sure you really want me?
all of a sudden   i had to pee
my nerves got the better, you see
an eighty-year-old married woman
decides she wants a boy toy;
i'm now in my late seventies
if younger   i'd do it with joy
but to be honest, i'm tired,
i'm really such a bore

my hormones
don't like to be stirred anymore

5 - one hour with tina

she walks into my store one day
divorced, alone, left with two kids
strikingly beautiful, dirty blond hair
we start to talk small talk
then she spoke of her life–
survivor of an abusive, controlling husband
a teen romance of love led to parenthood
now educated
self-aware
she couldn't take his dominance anymore
had to find herself
broke free
fifty-three
looks like twenty
you're well preserved   i told her,
while she thinks for a minute
to decide on an expensive purchase

finally, she bought one
then left the store
and a memory

poetry community

proper poets place pronouns
correctly in a strict format
in traditionally written poems
with rhyme every time

beat poets
            don't
they write free form
let
    words
            and space
perform

use metaphors
    like semaphores
            to tell a story

finality

i see my grave
is already dug and waiting
wonder if god will dig me up
or do i remain worm food forever

as heaven passes overhead
   the living below
     will read my poems;
they'll say

too bad for him
his stuff is good
wonder what he was like

as they turn the page

you look pretty in green

blond hair
resting on verdant velour shoulders
pursed pink painted lips
blue sparkling sapphire eyes
i saw her in a mall store
as she tried on a man's suit
too shy to approach her

she has a fashion model aura
in a new jersey men's store
on a weekday evening

while by the center court fountain
round girls with a too-tight top
have a boy's hand
in their back pocket
squeezing
and kissing a thick, layered neck

while i'm staring at perfection
with my hands in my pockets
praying, wishing,
for a dream to come true

rehab

spent a college education
six times over
on rehabs
trying to get her sober
addiction is hard to kick
a free state-run inner city one
was the last place she went
the minority roommate
with a four-inch scar
on her left cheek
looked at her
touch my stuff i'll fuck'n kill youse
is   a nice to meet you   greeting
tragically, that was way better
than the food

nobody there ate anyway
track-marks shout out
eating is not necessary
when you have sweats and shakes

please get me out of here
four days later, she left,
weeks ahead of schedule
suburban girls are lunch meat there

what was her name again?

it was our first date
i took her out to eat
then was disappointed
she refused to rub my feet

i did take off my shoes
and wore freshly laundered socks
unfortunately, she refused
she said she was so confused

a low-cut dress exposed
two in front   of my nose
i thought i'd take things slow
but she was set to go

we jumped into bed
she started with my head
luckily, i have two

god!   i almost died

autumn leaves

on my walk today i saw a tall tree
outstretched limbs almost bare
piles of fallen red and gold
raked in piles at its base

on the upper branches
a small bunch hung tight
fighting coming winter freeze
as they cling dearly to their youth

my neighbor is near her trail's end
facial trenches and jowls
surgically gone, with crow's feet
pulled up disfiguring crystal blue eyes

tight tops, leggings, and colorful
clothes try to resurrect youth
until the endless march of life loosens its grip,
then all the leaves will finally fall

dinner one night

at the warehouse food court
she sat diagonally to my right,
her back to me,
i see her left arm and hands
are covered in tattoos

her wire rim glasses
give a hippie poetic aura
as her brown hair is pulled back
into a ponytail,
and her body, slim, in
jeans and blouse casually cool

when i leave and look back
i realize she could be typecast
as a muse in poetry or art
yet here she is eating a dollar-fifty hot dog

in manhattan
a coffee house is missing its poet
an empty stage with
people waiting for readings to start,
while in new jersey
a foot long in a roll is devoured

hands

hands are everywhere
usually, they come in pairs
one on each arm
one on each side
they grasp, grip, grope
they hold other's hands in love
whether dry or sweaty
their digits on the end
come in useful, on occasion,
to do mundane everyday things
yet hands are most valued
when they tender touch

abortion in america

regarding qualifications
for political office,
in most states
you don't need the following:
a high school degree,
the ability to read, write,
or reason, and even do
simple arithmetic;
but you do need to win a
popularity contest
called an election

doctor oz,
a gubernatorial candidate
in pennsylvannia,
said *abortion*
should be between a woman,
her doctor, and local politicians

welcome to alice's wonderland
where up is down
and we are living in it,
it is called america

i've had enough

i am tired of the bullshit
life throws at people
stupid rules
stupid regulations
due to job justifications
which make no sense
but we have to obey
many of us have no say
in their formulation
to strip pretense away
of lies and degradation–
let us lay naked
on a nude beach
to let it all hang out
and make exciting love
till dawn or exhaustion
or police enforce
some regulation

individual rights

thin-lipped people
on the mayflower
were immigrants
came on several sailing ships
to enjoy life, liberty and
religious freedom;
today far-right politicians
        want every person
to follow **their** religious beliefs
about women's bodies and medical procedures
no matter where they came from
or what they believe,
thick lips, thin lips, or no lips
individual rights are constricted
by conservative, bigoted, misogynist
politicians in america

overcoming adversity

greeted at the car dealership
a young woman
at the front desk
cheerily
offers to assist
she calls a salesperson

after minutes of banter
we have a moment
made a later lunch date
i look forward to it

not a breathtaking beauty
her vitality shines
becomes irresistible
men are charmed
beyond reason

suitors smitten
nobody notices shiny braces
to enable feeble legs
to stand
to walk
with a cane's help

death of a tree

it reached way past its teen years
my house was built
twenty-seven years ago
the lone fruitless pear tree
probably planted then

its roots wound around
its trunk

when planted
the hole was not dug deep
burlap wrap not cut
it didn't grow healthy

today the arborist came
its stump ground down
only my memory of it
still stands tall

sorry about hymie town

no, i don't accept the apology
because everyone has a bias
some like sweet mustard
some like spicy
yet when it comes to people
they are all colors and kinds
and i accept, as fact,
most folks have a preference;
but intelligent people
keep it to themselves, in silence,
because we all need to live together
so no, i don't accept the apology

museum portraits

the oil paintings hang on a museum's bland wall
they're of dead people sitting stiff and tall
the ones on the left are rich and noble
with fine silken clothes and a blank facial gaze

no one smiles, even with a pet on their lap
small children stand rigid right next to a chair
the wives look dower as they sit or stand
while across the hall, everyone has some fun

those pictures are of cherubic, laughing nude
women
cavorting on lawns or wading in ponds
while the well-dressed men look from across the
room
now realize why their wives don't smile anymore

they know the parties over there
all they can do now is just sit and stare

seasons

i used to enjoy seasonal changes
in my youth,

spring smells of fresh flowers
romp 'round with friends
was so delightful;
now, most are dead

in summer, my family spent
warmest months on a farm;
i explored barns and cows
and swam in a forested creek
as ice water from the stream
splashed on my body   i was alive

autumn brought school days,
long hours, an elderly, dreary teacher
only the blond girl i sat next to,
brightened the day, she was friendly,
very friendly, in the back row with me

now in the winter of my life
the year is ending
only memories exist
tomorrow is a gamble i play every night
and sunrise   is the winning jackpot

vietnam memorial washington d.c.

polished black granite
slices into the ground
fifty thousand names
of those who served
and died
chiseled in it
a reminder of war's futility
a reminder of lost futures
this is the parade of honor
for those who came back
never had

incongruous

artists are renowned
for being with a muse
to paint them
dressed   or   undressed
standing   or   lying down
with others   or   alone
yet poets cannot write of them
without walking a fine line–
today instant information
can signal sexual transgressions
whether real or imagined   isn't important
morals can be impugned   or imposed
because of society's sexual sensibilities
rightful or not–
today's muses are literary orphans
secret sexual sycophants
to be loved in darkness
away from prying eyes   and readers

lithuania

in this small baltic nation
there once was a forest
in and near vilnius
of sixty thousand jewish trees
whose roots were hundreds of centuries deep
birthing a bloom of intellect,
poetry, literature, and learning
that spread to every continent–
although almost every tree is cut down,
burned, buried, and chopped to pieces
their roots are deep
their branches spread
the trees are reborn
elsewhere in the world
and they flourish again

with you

everything and nothing
we spoke for hours
the conversation didn't matter
    we were together

hearts spoke in silence
    to be near you
    to see you
    to be in your presence

love is funny like that
it's not physical all the time
your being completes me

i need to be yours forever

manhattan chestnuts 1954

it was christmas week, my parents took
my sister and i to see the tree at rockefeller center-
why, i don't know, but it was cold

an artic wind blew down the avenue
as broad brick buildings
acted like a fuel funnel

wind, strong winds,
i walked between a group
of tall adults to block it,
but cold and windy,
the wind never stopped

my toes and fingers froze
when my father stopped
at a sidewalk stand, he bought
a bag of freshly roasted chestnuts

the hot bag warmed my hands, the nuts tasted ok,
i never had them before; i couldn't keep my fingers in
there long enough since my kid sister
insisted on having some too,
inconsiderate little thing

i don't remember the tree or anything else that night,
except the warmth the chestnuts gave,
i fell asleep
in the car ride back to brooklyn, finally

death

there is an absolute in life
no one can avoid
we're all finite, and
will fade into the night
to all   out of sight
and eventually, be forgotten-
only in writing can we live on;
our thoughts, dreams, and goals
can again be lived by others
vicariously
if you take the time
to write them
before the earth
falls into the sun

mornings bring a darkness

it's a countdown
to eternity as
god ticks off
merits and demerits
while lilith
cuddles me to her chest
embraces my soul with temptations
and engorges herself
on my body

i am left shattered
and shameless
only to wearily leave my bed,
and her,
to task myself with career,
and return
while she waits
impatiently at home

wintry mess

i met her in summer long ago
kindhearted, warm, charismatic
many boys constantly pursued her
then she decided on one to date

bad boys have an unhealthy allure
touch a hot stove; you'll get burned–
there are some people you stay away from;
sadly, we too often learn from experience

their marriage was terrible
in the winter of their union
violence and virulent vitriol occurred
it stopped after a divorce and prison

winter

winter blankets
wool winter blankets
warm woolen winter blankets
when it's freezing outside
warm woolen winter blankets
will warm like toast
when you worm yourself inside
wrapped in a warm woolen blanket

jersey mall hat store sale

red hats are on sale
too many people voted them out
nobody wants them anymore
they are the red capes
the matador waved
to his huggish horned bulls
who tried to destroy democracy
available in all brain sizes
especially extra small

in the news

madness
hate rages
innocents killed
it was a safe space
club q violated
patrons shot and killed
rath, bigotry
no reason
love died
tears

parades

i watch the thanksgiving day parade
with all the pretty things to see
floats, balloons, dancers, and girls twirl
it seems similar to a person's life
as they pass by
none of the nice things last
they'll be gone soon too

found only in memories

cash five lottery

the rain stopped last night
rays of sun shined in the window;
it's thanksgiving
i felt lucky
the dollar lottery's up to
$665,422–
drove to the liquor store
bought five tickets
the man said *good luck*–
in my bones, i felt lucky too–
later, family came for dinner
i never mentioned the tickets
when the turkey was served
i imagine how i'd spend the money–
new cars, clothes, all the adult toys
my heart desired; later,
with intense anticipation,
i spread out five tickets
and start to check numbers–
none on the first
one on the second
none on the third
one on the fourth
then i check the fifth and final ticket–
there are days in everyone's life
that is sweet, pleasant, and prosperous;
this was not one of them

finality

got a call this morning
told me of my friend's death
on saturday

he took a shower   and
dropped dead on the floor
seventy-seven   my age too
yet i'm here   and he's not
don't know if there's a place to go
once you're gone
no one's returned
no postcards
or letters   from there
i'm pretty sure there is no there
or a second chance
to come back from

when it's my turn
i hope it's fast
just dig a hole
and throw me in
then read a poem
of flowers and sun

questions

today i read about autochromes;
old pictures from 1903 that are
light-sensitive and rarely shown

one is of a mother and infant
i wonder what became of the baby
reaching maturity in the roaring 1920's

of the mother who tenderly
looked down at her child, wrapped
in white, with clear silken skin

a century passed, world wars fought,
millions died needlessly; has there been progress-
i wonder what happened to this innocent baby

second amendment

how does it end
not when
but how–
gun deaths stagger the imagination
children, parents, lovers
weddings postponed–
grave diggers become
a growth career
thanks to fetid, feckless politicians
morbid men make millions
making guns
making widows
making your beloved
wait to die
in supposedly safe everyday places

it's just money

i've made a lot
i've lost a lot
it's just money
it comes and goes
permanence sought, but
emotions last forever
once love is earned
it can be misspent
love has a value
worth more than money
remember
it's just money
not love

happy holiday

many people celebrate
many holidays
they give presents
they receive presents
almost every month has one
yet to me, there is only one holiday
it comes every day
when i see my child
every morning
every day
at home
not in the hospital
and i get
a big smile
a big hug
and can hold my child
in my arms
every day

long run

ahead
i see the end of the race
my heart pounds
hard deep breaths
can't get enough oxygen

it's been a great sprint
accomplished my goals
my feet are cold
at night
wool socks don't help
my valves leak
arteries calcified

i'm tired of this pace
soon my race will end
it'll be time to stop
my run'll be over
then i can rest
forever

inanimate objects

flower pots
on the shelf
he paints pink petals,
red and blue too

too many flowers
for too many buyers
for too many years
he pelted paint on canvas

enough!
he erupted
then decided
to now paint nudes

his wife agreed
to pose for him–
things equal to the same thing
are equal to each other

ordained

ungodly men of god
sinners of lust and avarice
different faiths
same faults
poisoned fruits
they mouth holy words
speak of holy deeds
as their flock blindly follows
while satan and lilith laugh
at this foolhardy folly

a gift

the longest moment
of her life
it lasted for seconds
yet stayed for years

he left next morning
forgot her name
his gift
hung around her neck

like an albatross
it saddled her
with debt and responsibility
for untold years

until old age
was she able to appreciate
the preciousness
of that longest moment

watermelon sale

the large red brick market
with two entrances on u.s. rt. 9
in new jersey
has a huge, lone, glass window
next to the main entry
with a blue neon sign flashing
watermelons!   watermelons!
as the fall food frenzy starts
with the anticipation of higher prices
since the growing season has ended–
the robust green ones are all gone
only the older, smaller, shriveled ones
remain
i gather together my resources
and make a purchase
then decide
how i am going to give out
my slices of watermelon
to heirs, friends, and charities

undertakers

they drive luxury sedans
colored in heartbroken black–
when called, they arrive
with long, dower faces

they park the hearse
then go inside
to soon come out
with a closed black bag;
inside is a hidden, cold corpse
to be prepared for final interment

it's a career comprised
of concern and compassion, you see,
not a jovial job for faint of heart
eventually   they will come for me

north atlantic summer cruise

the ocean between england
and the united states
is commonly called a pond
but this is not smooth water
as a woman's bath might be

curves of cascading crashing waves
smash down
to shake the sturdiest ships
while schools of dolphins
effortlessly
breach the surface
as they plow through
rough water ten feet high
in search of food

i turn to my left
see the ship's buffet
overwhelmed
by pods of bloated elderly whales
piling food high on plates

luck is

surviving pandemics
until a vaccine is approved
and not joining millions
who died before their time

coming home today
from a doctor's visit, after a
positive covid test, and able
to take a nap in my own bed

live long enough to have
two vaccines, four boosters,
and still breathe without a
ventilator in a hospital bed

to my family and friends
who haven't had a vaccine
i love you, and it's time
to get the damn shot already

luck is

call her rhapsody

she lives dangerously
body covered in colorful tattoos
lungs blackened
filled with smoke
drinks full bottles of liquor
dances all night
accepts cash
as she dips and bends
then grinds men's laps
as hands wander over tats
goes commando every day
loves to love in every way
always ready
to engage and engorge

crowded

in old age i look around and notice
my boyhood friends are missing
some moved far away
some only moved blocks
some moved permanently
         to somewhere i don't know
         forever lost

those who died
either went to hell
         as they did in life
others went to heaven, i guess,
but this i do know
         both places are very crowded

hatred

why!
why hate?
millions of patriots died
to defend everyone's rights
to live their life as they want
no matter
    religion
    skin color
    political beliefs
every mother loves their child
none want them killed or maimed needlessly

to be a good american citizen
you need to have
love and understanding,
compassion, humility, and charity

too soon

he died suddenly
my friend's death was untimely
i think they all are

one night in washington cemetery

i told her we'd marry
hands behind my back
two fingers crossed
i hoped to dally

cemetery's empty
no lights   except the moon
i lifted her up
to lay on his tomb
the dead would clap
     for us, if they could
it's been many long years
since a woman would moan

city rats scattered
scampered away
as we warmed the cold stone
until exhausted and spent
on a final resting place
in brooklyn that night

a city bus passed
the black iron gates
people would look in
the darkest midnight
while i gathered our clothes
and got ready to leave

old man shapiro
never had it so good
silent forever   below in his crypt
secrets not told   even if he could

after midnight

in manhattan, when the sun sets
on desolate side streets, it's deathly quiet
except for the straggler who walks home,
late, after a night out with friends, as
a taxi cruises past, seeking a fare

i peer out my apartment window
since sleep slipped away, insomnia rules my life
flashes of lightning slice through blackness
thunder booms, echoes bounce off endless
skyscrapers
in the valleys of the city; tiny droplets of rain
dot my glass, blur my vision; slowly,
i slightly open the window, smell the storm,
gusts of wind as it blows the street clean,
barely can see the man across the way
who walks faster, *bent forward* into the torrent

a wall of water glides up to him
as a raging river roars
to the garbage-blocked corner sewer
floods the intersection; a cab stops by my
building
and a woman gets out, loses a shoe when she
steps in the rushing water, watches it float
under a parked car, limps to the front awning,
disappears

i close my window and snuggle under a blanket,
rest on the pillow, close my eyes,
listen to the rhythmic tap, tap, tap
on top of the bedroom air conditioner
as the storm lulls me off to dreamworld

i have seen the rocky mountains

i stand next to them and look up
i drive into them, and on them,
they are large, high, massive
an american treasure to be savored
to look east from them
onto an unending-great-plains
as far as a person can see
my eyes see nothing but nature;
bison grazing, birds hunting,
fields upon fields of empty
unhampered in its beauty
not soiled by avarice
left alone as it has been for eons
i felt humble and insignificant

stranded

early september,
overcast sky
the rain starts,
more than a constant drizzle
not a downpour
as in a thunderstorm,
laura took the car to attend yoga class–
we live in a senior development
located in a rural area
with all of humanity's needs
a fifteen-minute car ride away–
my body is withdrawing
from chocolate;
she hid the sweets before she left,
i think she thrives on my diet discomfort–
there is a sense of wanting i cannot control,
yet i'm stranded on a barren island
surrounded by nothing,
an inability to get off it–
am i secretly on a reality television show

the trip

my granddaughter's carsick
as traffic crawls on the interstate
she grabs a barf bag mom
brought home from the hospital

the air conditioning
is turned up
past normal,
past high,
to maximum,

it doesn't help
uh oh,
now everyone's nauseous

maine is so far

just like elvis

when my mother
told me something
as a young child,
i always believed her

fawns follow a doe
for food and safety
there aren't second guesses,
they just do it
but teens
have a different viewpoint;
doubts exist
until proven otherwise

at the supermarket today
in the fine frozen foods section
i saw banana slices
covered with peanut butter
and encased in dark rich chocolate

it reminded me
of the sandwich elvis liked;
banana and peanut butter
on white bread

i bought it
tried it
ate it
tried it again
ate it again
elvis was right,
just like mom

helpers

lower manhattan streets
are narrow and curved
remnants of new amsterdam
when dutch held sway
yet today
they gather flocks of hurried walkers
who gawk at the pretty people
on their way to work or lunch
while girls in short skirts
are fancy flowers at the front desk
employed by wealthy businessmen
who fly them to distant meetings
as secretaries
though they can't do shorthand or type
but their assets keep them at work
while they stay silent
to enjoy the perks of gourmet dinners,
lush hotels, and all-expense-paid travels
far from spousal questions

chattanooga girl

i'm a wim-mins libber
with a six-barrel gun
waitin' at the depot
the train's runnin' late

you took my love
then threw it away
i took our baby
cause you're too crazy

things warmed up
with too much beer
doubt it will melt
your ice-cold heart
ain't the good ol' days
where you hit and run

you think you're so smart
now watch me depart
i'm headin' to nashville
you can keep your friends
gonna make it singing
cause my star's rising

i took our baby
you tore my heart apart
all i did
was love you
now watch as
the train departs

hotel room

always neat
always smells great
everything in its place
a temporary use
    not permanent

used

like you used me
    to satisfy your needs

not mine

i'm a brick house
built for permanence
not a hotel room she said

poets are different

i think there are two
types of poets today,
which one are you

the writer of wordplay
known as traditional, with
formats such as a b a b

or free verse, beat, or prose
phrases with rhythm and synonyms
format free using space
                          and lines
not restrained,
                  to write a
                              b
                                c
                                  d

time

runs
runs, runs,
can't reverse
always continues
i can't keep it, valuable
it slips through my life without STOP
it remains in memory
back occasionally
to be treasured
then forgot
misplaced
forever
gone
gone
gone

summer day at the beach

the heavy wool blanket is laid out
my wallet, in a plastic bag, buried
in the sand under a corner–
lotion smeared over my body
i lie down to stare up
as the white powder puffs pass
aimlessly, it seems, overhead–
i know they traveled from Chicago
to look down
at a deep-dish pizza eaten outside
on a sidewalk table– not inside,
by two lovers with olive oil fingers–
then floats over a farm in indiana
to watch a pig farmer
throw food scraps on the ground
for the fat sow and mud-covered piglets–
in pennsylvannia as it stood
over the capital
to watch a republican official
place an envelope in his jacket pocket
as a lobbyist walks away smiling–
finally, it arrives over my blanket,
as sunshine streaks down
to broil me alive
while clouds gently glide away
on their way
to watch whales at sea

and my life goes on

cfc furniture

almost forty years ago
closed the family business
     after three generations
sold the brooklyn building,
sold off the inventory,
emptied everything else,
locked the door, walked away,
kept only one thing of value

to me

a stainless-steel letter opener
about one inch wide, heavy,
a blunted point after years of
use and abuse, with
heavy morrocan scrolling on the handle –

when
i place it in my hand
i can feel my father's presence
i can hear my father's voice
i can sense my grandfather
     hold this in his aged hand
     as he did over seventy-five years ago –
everything has an ending
it was not easy to stop
a generational business
and restart elsewhere,
because life continues

that thigh - a modern sonnet

that thigh,
i don't know why
i'd like to climb high
he said with a sigh
maybe he needs
some whisky and rye
yet he knew if he did
he'd certainly die
with a smile on his face
and not a disgrace
he'd go from a zero
to a big-time hero

oh, to die
in a lovely thigh

restroom at a rest stop

the old vauxhall road rest stop
on the garden state parkway
was an experience in grunge

men's room had stalls with doors
but didn't lock, fruit flies buzz in them,
graffiti on walls, and when you

enter, stench is overbearing
as men at the urinals stand there,
and turn, exposed, to meet guys

ugh

hundreds of roadway miles top-notch,
maintained, snow and ice removed,
yet they can't clean up a restroom

funeral procession

her coffin drawn by horses
grenadier guards
dress in regal red
with tall black bear fur hats
walk   slowly   alongside

the queen's purple crown
emblazoned
with thousands of diamonds
sits above the casket
over a royal flag

the question is
why don't poets deserve similar–
devoted publishers could walk alongside
with published poetry books stacked high
on top of the casket
legions of librarians lead the way
news shows report it
people cry in the streets
a great poet has passed
readers are bereft
only his books are left

almost

i'm riding the subway to manhattan-
outside,
a heavy drizzle smears itself on the windows
as the train speeds toward the next stop-
inside, i see a young woman with freckles,
tiny brown dots on her cheeks
and across the bridge of her nose,
her red hair rests on a green linen blouse-
we smile at each other
the train continues to tumble
from side to side
it races under the east river; i hold
on to the vertical chrome bar,
she is on the other side
trying not to fall, and smiling at me;
a fast turn, everyone shifts about
i catch her in my arms-
she doesn't move away or say anything,
i lower my head slightly
as she raises hers, our eyes are inches away;
at that moment,
the train enters the station
she says goodbye with a smile

picture album

my wedding album is thick and heavy
with thirty-six,
eight-by-ten color pictures
bound in heavy clear plastic
of one hundred and
fifty family and friends;
fifty-four years later, i can
recognize almost everyone pictured
frozen in time as they stand   smiling,
or hold a drink in their hand   as they sit
at tables of ten, crammed together, the
women wear white fancy dresses
in style back then,
now second-hand consignment shop goods–
the anecdotes of their lives flood my memory,
smiles and tears are nonstop
as i turn the pages–
when i look closer, realize,
the ones still alive can be counted on fingers,
toes not needed–
i close the book
yet they still talk to me
to haunt my life decisions

humor

i remember as a little boy
my parents went to the mountains
for a two-week hotel vacation
and took me along–
my mother and aunt decided one day
to go for a walk;
as i schlepped along a mountain road
we all heard my father's belly laugh
echo   from the valley below

i see humor in almost everything,
like dad, and my youngest son
inherited the gift too; he performed
standup comedy in manhattan
for many years

when dad died,
my five-year-old daughter asked
if he died from laughing too much;
i thought it was a great way
to be remembered

that thing of hers

she values this item
hidden unseen in drawers
    he gifted it to her–
it's not expensive to buy
she could have bought it herself
although it gives great pleasure
those times she is alone at night
thinking of him, away from her,
yet still intimate

i remember family dinners

mom cooking at the stove
dad sitting to my right
and sister at the other end

the birthday cakes and candles
holiday dinners with grandparents
breakfast with glass bottled milk
cold, poured over cereal

the day my beloved grandmother
died, and grandpa moved in,
he took my sister's seat at the table;
she took her food upstairs
'cause he ate with his mouth open

so many things happened
at that cramped small table
today i have my own family,
sister lives a thousand miles away
in a damp, humid, hot state
within spitting distance to cuba;
everyone else is dead

scared of mia

he has a cicatrix
on his chest
to mark the spot
where a heart
used to be
after he willfully
tore hers out
and left a bundle
of flesh
sobbing on the floor
and decided
     after a long courtship
he was not happy
with a latina woman
who loved him
completely
     asshole

closed

when a synagogue closes
it is worse than a tragedy
it is a generational death
not a single death, it is the
death of a jewish community

on the high holidays
when the shofar sounds
the ghosts
of those who prayed there rise
to remember the simchas
and the memorial kaddish
many recited over the years

the building is now empty,
sometimes torn down
sometimes used for other purposes
yet in the memories of past members
it still lives on

a poet's tombstone

too many consonants did him in
counting syllables was his sin
all his life, he loved to rhyme
he ran out of lines   it was his time

mom's cooking

my mother's brisket had
onions, chicken fat, and
tasted fabulous, served on
holidays for guests
every year, it
remains in my memory forever

friendship

in youth, we schooled together
played in the streets together,
and in bands, as we grew up–
we planned to be together,
buddies forever in life–
last year i bought two rockers
for my front porch
so we can sit and still sing
side by side
as the clouds fly silently overhead
while we remember memories
in our old age; but a car wreck
ended him at twenty,
now at seventy
i sit alone

bees

the self-righteous, rigid religious
are over there
right there
there   see them
like honey bees
they hover over flowers
everyone's flowers–
they want to take the pollen,
their pollen,
their way,
not allow other bees to fly freely
prevent them from pollinating as they desire,
as they want or not, and
go to other flower beds instead

every other bee has to live
in their imagined holy nests
because they are the only,
right,
kind of bee

ronettes

where'd ya go ronnie
i miss the harmony
to feel the beat with my feet
i want to be your baby

you're gone from the airwaves
yet remain on my round, plastic, forty-five
in a cardboard case standing upright
while i remain prostrate on my bed

1963 forever lives in my memory, and
on oldies request days since i no longer own
a round table and speaker; ronnie
i want to be your baby

to write a poem

use your whole being
then jump into the abyss
you know your destination
experience the journey
as you go
            deeper
                    and deeper
exploring crevices of your mind

the hand

still strong
it used to have
a steel-like vise grip
sturdy and steady;
now, not so much–
still can hold a straight razor
but can't use it properly
tremors
tremors
make it a useless appendage
something to fill a shirt sleeve with
and is able to put a pencil
between fingers
but can't legibly write
or touch the correct keyboard letter;
a body born years ago
with unlimited physical potential

now disabled

yet still has an exceptional mind

doctor-patient reality

the pretty twenty-something young nurse
with chestnut eyes, thick black hair, and a skin-
tight top
leads me into a tiny pale blue exam room,
instructs
me to completely undress and put on a paper
gown
before she smiles and says *the doctor will be
right in*

as i sit on the examining table, waiting,
the air conditioner starts;
the vent in the ceiling above my head
blows down ice-cold air cause goosebumps
luckily, i still had on thick socks
my toes won't get frostbite

the doctor walks in and asks me what i'm there
for, looks at me for sixty seconds, then sits on
a basic backless black stool in front of a
computer screen and types, types, and types
some more before telling me a prescription is
now sent to my pharmacy

on the way out to the front desk to pay my co-
pay
i thank the computer screen for helping me get
better

wall street bigot 1968

in nineteen seventy, i worked
as an over-the-counter trader
at eighty pine street in manhattan
for a few months after my marriage

the company leased two full floors
in the building before they merged
with another even larger firm on wall street-
back then, it was a major company

on the trading desk, there were about
forty men, none older than thirty-five,
and i was one of the younger traders
at twenty-two, and the only college graduate

one tuesday morning, the irish vice president
fired
all four jewish traders in his department;
considering
there were only four on our floor, and six total
in the whole company, and no minorities of color,
it says a lot about diversity

yankee stadium 1961

i was a brooklyn dodger fan–
in my teenage mind
the bronx bombers sucked
although they won a lot of games
the stadium is where "they" play
i couldn't care less if they won
but my buddies wanted to go

trains took forever from newkirk station–
we walked through the hallowed stadium
where legends of the game played–
then sat in the right field bleachers
and the soft hum of the crowd erupted
when yogi came to pinch hit

sitting there felt funny, emmet kelly
was missing from the pitcher's mound;
only in ebbits field can you find a
famous ringling brothers circus clown
entertaining thousands of laughing fans–
not today, not here, in old, staid, yankee stadium
bereft of a *wait till next year crowd*

one finger

we have
ten to choose
                 two are problematic
each hand
has one

in new york, the middle finger
flies like a bird when angered
a meaning understood
(expletive deleted)

point the pointer finger
in a public school
and a fight breaks out
my momma ain't dead
is the war cry before fists fly

a thumb up is okay
it's good; it's the way
to a shortcut to approval
no words needed to say

the ring finger and pinky
are just there
like millions of seen and unheard
who go about their lives
morning till night
doing,
just doing

orange groves

smudge pots burn bright in my mind
yet my fingers and toes freeze
the clogged blue rivers carry my blood
away
away from a leaking pump
straining
straining to carry life through a body
weary, worn down by decades
weary with irreplaceable parts

worn out

soon the hot pots
will extinguish
and the frost will win
the brightness will dull at dusk
welcoming the forever night

wedding band

originally it was gold
with fine etchings all around
an inscription on the inner band
a marriage date dug deep into it
with the word *forever*

after decades have past
she still has it, secured,
it's kept in a sock drawer
too heavy to wear
it turned to lead
after he left her

acirema, my country?

america is upside down, backword crazy;
a proud political party
once stood for individual rights
against big government
now it has politicians standing
in private exam rooms with doctors
to determine if a medical procedure
can proceed, or to criminalize a doctor

the right to vote, once the backbone
of our democracy and fought for,
is now blocked by those same politicians;
republican legislatures want to negate
a popular vote if it doesn't go its way–
hello, third-world dictatorships, open
your doors, acirema is knocking

redemption

she was born an innocent
the future filled with opportunity
a bud growing,
nurtured to blossom
bright and lively,
her charisma overflows
her teen years welcomed the devil
party time with drugs
and two friends when
one died at twenty,
the other disappeared–
no college education,
the money spent on rehabs
thirty days in,
    sixty out,
thirty days back again
a never-ending spiral
for twenty plus years
finally took it seriously
with twelve step meetings
now her flower blooms
with a sweet fragrance
once more

a visit to cuba

the streets of old havana greet me–
my spanish blood, long dormant and diminutive,
sizzles; estoy en casa ahora echoes in my soul–
i walk down a narrow valley
of faded pastel-colored buildings in pink, blue,
and sun-bleached green–
i pass nineteen fifties red chevrolets, blue fords,
and an early sixties white cadillac
with high rear tail fins and a rojo leather interior–
the driver in the parked car lights a thick,
long-leaf cuban cigar, then exhales the classic
smell of historic cuba– the chica who sits next to
him wears an off-the-shoulder blouse, and with
one finger
twirls it in his slicked-back black hair– soon, the
cruise ship will leave and take me back to new
jersey with my friend fernando's jewels– he can
never return to what was to be a people's
paradise of equality and prosperity, and his
beloved homeland– years ago, before he became
a political prisoner of fidel, he buried them, and
asked me to dig them up at his madre's grave

nostalgia

sometimes i dream of the old days,
to go back to when things were sweet and
everybody was pleasant and had manners,
and crime was only in day-old newspapers

food tasted much better years ago
apples had a good crunch, didn't rot so fast,
chemical additives killed the bugs and us,
but we died with a full stomach, satiated

girls smiled and waited till marriage
except for those kinds   who lived over there-
jobs were plentiful, and the president
inspired and not divided us by hate speech

today, i am informed about things that happened
in minutes, and what is going to happen, and
as soon as someone does something; if only
i could have a rest-full full night's sleep, again

stanzas

if only life were like a poem–
the words we speak
sentences we create
would flow into stanzas
to be moved about
when needed,
or put to the side
for when we decide
to get back to it
    or even deleted–
reality is permanent,
what we said or did
can't be moved to tomorrow;
we can't take it back,
our words and actions live forever–
if only life is like a poem

scary night

it is all-hallows eve
tricksters gather in force
screams leave them hoarse
their goal to instill freight

after dusk, the ghouls come out
vampires wake and open their tombs
blood lures them tonight. it's time to eat
live bodies are a midnight treat

the living dead have left their bed
trick or treat is what's always said
arms outstretched, they ring your bell
it's candy they want, or they'll raise hell

a thought about poets

pity poor poets
never rich
they write and write
and color watermelons
blue with purple fruit
using metaphors
to paint with words
then starve
as artists have done before

a truism
poets are wealthy
not with money or stocks
but rich in creativity

mom's cooking

there are some things
a person remembers
like how thin
they used to be in youth
i know mine
is because of her cooking skills
or maybe
a lack of them too

a minute steak takes a minute
to cook till ready to serve
in 1950's, back then,
she created cajun blackened cooking
when ten minutes
was the minimum time

there was no blood,
stiff as a mafia hit
and just as dead
with no flexibility

no wonder i was underweight
she lovingly starved me for years
thank-goodness for oreo cookies
a row with cold milk was dinner
a row with cold milk was lunch
a row with cold milk was breakfast
and a tuna sandwich after school
from a coffee shop, famous in the city

a girl from somerset

music starts,
doors open
ahead   i see my bride
my commitment, and
my sister's friend
who made the introduction

yes, the one
who introduced me to a past love
the narcissistic american teen beauty queen
who cheated on her steady boyfriend
    with me
one christmas years ago
stunning
she embraced life to the fullest
in an exciting way
yet not someone to build a future with
only a fond memory

Flash Fiction

Buying a car

One evening, I stopped at a car dealership to buy a car for my grandson. A pretty Latina receptionist at the front desk wore a low-cut dress exposing her fullness, greeted me with a beautiful smile, and introduced herself, then asked if I needed help.

I requested a salesperson, and she dutifully paged one. While I waited, we started to talk, and I told her I write poetry books and asked if she was a reader. After I handed her one of my cards, we spoke for a few minutes more until a saleslady walked over. In those few minutes, I felt we had a special moment together.

An hour or so later, I bought the car.

On my way out, she passed by me and said goodbye with her warm smile "feel free to stop in to see me anytime you are in the area," she said.

Three days later, the license plates came in, and I visited the dealership to pick them up.

She was again at the front desk and smiled when I approached the reception area.

"Nice to see you again," she said.

"Yes, I'm here to get my plates for the car."

"Okay, I'll get them for you; what is your name again?"

"I thought we had a moment when we first met; you already forgot my name?"

She giggled.

"Give me your hand," I said.

I extended my right one, and she placed hers on top, then I placed my left one over hers.

"My name is Elliot M. Rubin; I am a poet. I am also the greatest lover you never will have. If I were not married, I'd whisk you away to Las Vegas for a weekend of steak, nightclubs, and swimming, then drive out into the desert to a secluded spot and make love until you are exhausted. The next time you are in the arms of someone special, you'll remember my story of the trip we never took together, and you'll also remember my name is Elliot M. Rubin."

She laughed, then walked to the back to get my license plates.

Unfortunately, I don't remember her name!

the end

About the Author

elliot m rubin is an exciting american poet who has been in numerous anthologies and books of poems. His free verse style of writing is refreshing and easily understood.

to read more of the author's books of poetry, please check out this website: CreativeFiction.net

Thank you for reading my poetry

For other books of poetry written by me, please visit my personal website:

www.CreativeFiction.net

To follow me on Instagram, go to:

elliot_m_rubin

**all my books
are available online
from Amazon**